BR**O**WSE
Magazine

Cover Photo Credits: ©JKlingebiel/Shutterstock

Houghton
Mifflin
Harcourt

hmhco.com

UNIT 1

FACING FeaR

Phobias

Earthquakes

How to Say I'm Scared

The Challenge

Fears and Superstitions

Monsters That Need Help

Tips to Face Fear

UNIT 2

Animal Intelligence

Ivan the Gorilla ✳ Pigeons ✳ Whales and Dolphins ✳ Dogs ✳ Cephalopods

UNIT 3

UNIT 3

Dealing with DISASTER

Fire Safety

Volcanoes

Cities in Ruin

Shoking Movies

Emergency Plans

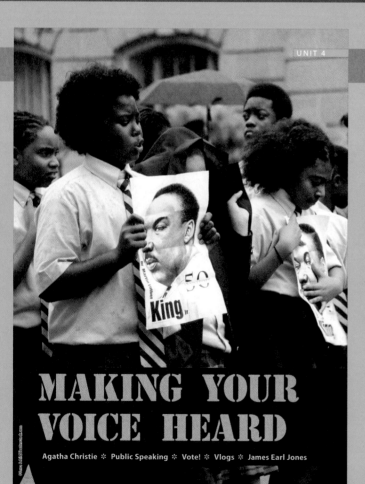

MAKING YOUR VOICE HEARD

Agatha Christie ❋ Public Speaking ❋ Vote! ❋ Vlogs ❋ James Earl Jones

vi

UNIT 4

UNIT 4

UNIT 5

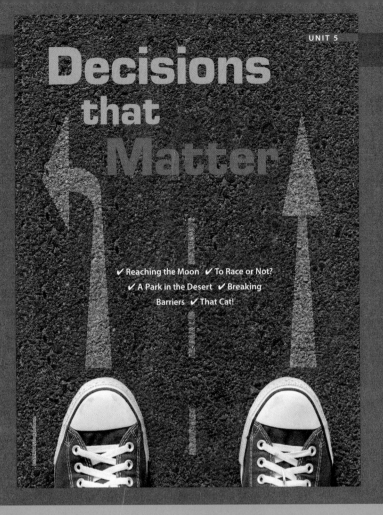

Decisions that Matter

UNIT 5

✔ Reaching the Moon ✔ To Race or Not?
✔ A Park in the Desert ✔ Breaking
Barriers ✔ That Cat!

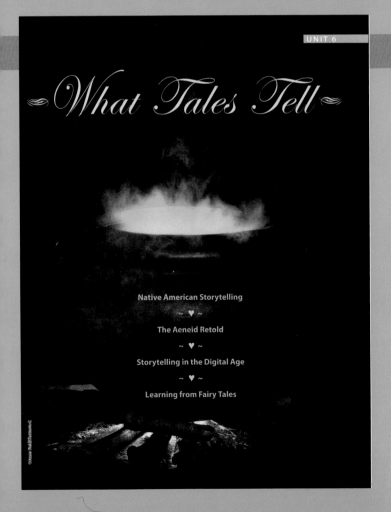

What Tales Tell

UNIT 6

Native American Storytelling

~ ♥ ~

The Aeneid Retold

~ ♥ ~

Storytelling in the Digital Age

~ ♥ ~

Learning from Fairy Tales

UNIT 6

Facing Fear

City Phobias

You don't want this office if you have **acrophobia,** the fear of heights.

If you have **dromophobia,** the fear of crossing streets, you might have to walk around and around the same block forever.

Not a good place to walk if you have **batophobia,** the fear of being close to tall buildings.

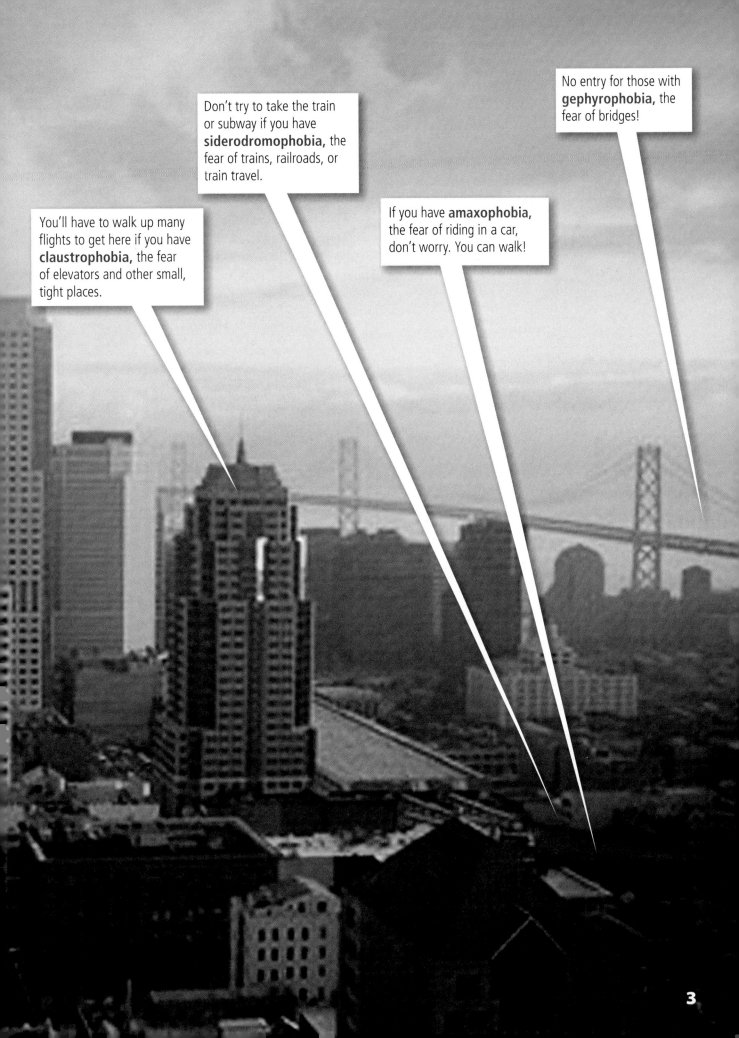

You'll have to walk up many flights to get here if you have **claustrophobia,** the fear of elevators and other small, tight places.

Don't try to take the train or subway if you have **siderodromophobia,** the fear of trains, railroads, or train travel.

If you have **amaxophobia,** the fear of riding in a car, don't worry. You can walk!

No entry for those with **gephyrophobia,** the fear of bridges!

Country Phobias

No cooling off in the lake or stream for you if you have **limnophobia,** the fear of lakes, or **potamophobia,** the fear of rivers or running water.

Who knows what might live in here? Stay clear if you have **herpetophobia,** the fear of reptiles or creepy, crawly things, or **entomophobia,** the fear of insects.

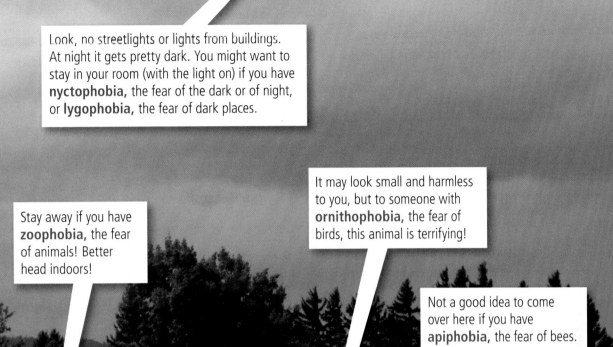

Look, no streetlights or lights from buildings. At night it gets pretty dark. You might want to stay in your room (with the light on) if you have **nyctophobia,** the fear of the dark or of night, or **lygophobia,** the fear of dark places.

It may look small and harmless to you, but to someone with **ornithophobia,** the fear of birds, this animal is terrifying!

Stay away if you have **zoophobia,** the fear of animals! Better head indoors!

Not a good idea to come over here if you have **apiphobia,** the fear of bees.

Earthquake Fear in California
and What Californians Are Doing About It!

by Mia Lewis

There have been many earthquakes in California over the years, both large and small. Scientists know that more are coming. The problem is, they don't know exactly when or where they will strike, or how serious they will be. California has various strategies to try to keep its residents safe.

Safety Is . . . Strong Buildings

If you are hoping to stay safe in an earthquake, it helps a lot if your house doesn't fall on top of you. It turns out that the best way to prevent people from getting hurt during an earthquake is to make sure the buildings where they live and work are strong enough to withstand an earthquake's worst moves.

New buildings in California follow **building codes** that have been designed to help them remain standing during earthquakes. Existing structures can be **retrofitted** so they are more likely to withstand an earthquake's shifts and shakes.

©Mark Downey/Getty Images

GET PREPARED!

Here are some precautions that help keep Californians safe.

- **Drop, Cover, and Hold On!** It's what you do when the earth is shaking. Drop down, take cover under something solid, like a sturdy table or desk, and hold on tight until the earth stops moving. Schoolchildren in California practice during regular earthquake drills.

- **Make Your House Earthquake-Ready.** Getting your house earthquake-ready means thinking ahead: bolting bookshelves to the wall so they can't fall on top of you; moving heavy glass mirrors so they aren't near a bed; installing latches on kitchen cupboards so plates and glasses can't fall out when the house is shaking.

- **Have an Emergency Kit Ready-Made.** In fact, have two: one for the car and one for the house. Kits should contain food and water; tools (a first-aid kit, flashlights and batteries, a radio, eating utensils, etcetera); clothes, blankets, and sturdy shoes.

- **Practice!** The Great ShakeOut earthquake drills give Californians a chance to take part in an earthquake readiness drill every year.

There's More Than One Way

by Felice Singer

Scared, terrified, frightened, petrified, afraid, fearful . . .

There are so many words to choose from when you want to express fear. There are also **idioms**.

An **idiom** is a group of words that means something different from what each word means on its own. Idioms can be colorful and fun. Look at the idioms highlighted in the story below and see if you can figure out what each of them means. Then check the chart on the next page to see if you were correct!

~~~~~~~~~~~~~~~~~~~~~~~~~

Scared Stiff

One day my neighbor Rickie asked me and my sister Soo-Lai to watch a movie. We said yes. Then Rickie told us the title: *Zombie Spider Explosion*. Soo-Lai cheered. My reaction was the opposite. I got **goose bumps** and **felt a knot** in my stomach. I tried to tell Rickie that horror movies were **not my cup of tea**. But before I could say anything, the lights went out and the movie started.

The idea of a movie about giant zombie spiders **scared me out of my wits**. Right from the start I was just one big **bundle of nerves**. As the scary music started, I **broke out in a cold sweat**.

I was **scared stiff** when the boy got trapped in the giant web. Then Soo-Lai dropped the remote on my leg and I **jumped out of my skin!** When the movie was finally over, I was **as white as a ghost**, and **quaking in my boots**.

~~~~~~~~~~~~~~~~~~~~~~~~~

Say You're Scared!

This . . . means THAT!

Idiom	Meaning
have a knot/sick feeling in the pit of your stomach	feel afraid, nervous, or anxious
goose bumps	bumps on the skin from fear, cold, or excitement
not your cup of tea	something you do not enjoy
a bundle of nerves	very nervous
scared out of your wits	to be very badly scared or frightened; to be terrified
scared stiff	so scared you may be unable to move
break out into a cold sweat	so scared or anxious that you begin to sweat
jump out of my skin	suddenly shocked, surprised, or startled
quake in my boots	tremble from fear
have nerves of steel	be very brave
turn white as a ghost	become pale due to shock or fear

FeaRSoMe FeaRs and

What do snakes, planes, bats, rats, spiders, lightning, the number 13, black crows, a haunted house, and aliens from outer space have in common?

They're all things that can create fear or discomfort in some people. Let's take a closer look at that list.

The mere sight of a snake can send shivers down the spine of millions. Why? Well, some psychologists believe that this fear may go back to a time when humans had to survive in the wild, a wild that included deadly snakes. To reassure anyone with that fear, the chance of being bitten by a venomous snake is slim, and we now have medicines to treat snakebites.

What about rats? Some of the fear of rats may also date back in history. Rats, or rather the fleas common to rodents such as rats, have often been blamed for causing plagues in the Middle Ages that killed millions. Scholars still debate about this, but meanwhile, many people would rather stay away from rats. Rats, by the way, are very intelligent. They can make great pets and can be very sociable and playful.

Some people find black crows frightening. Many cultures associate crows with death and dying. Crows feed on carrion, the flesh of the dead animals. But crows are highly intelligent birds. They're so smart that they can remember people's faces.

Then there are superstitions that make some people fearful. Take the number 13, for example. Some people believe it's unlucky. They may not like Friday the 13th, either!

SUPERSTITIONS

by Margaret Maugenest

Depending on where in the world you live, black cats signify either good or bad luck. In the United States, it may be considered bad luck if a black cat crosses your path. But in Japan, a black cat is considered lucky.

Halloween, the annual event where images thought to be frightful abound, would not look quite right without the spiders, spider webs, bats, and haunted houses.

Fears can have different origins and reasons. Take the fear of thunder and lightning. The sound of thunder caused by lightning can be frightening, but it won't hurt you. Lightning on the other hand can injure or kill. There is no safe place to be outside during thunderstorms. Remember: "When Thunder Roars, Go Indoors."

But what about the fear of flying? There are people who refuse to fly because they believe it may be dangerous. In fact, statistics concluded that flying was almost 30 times safer than driving!

There is one last fear on the list — that of the unknown. What's out there in outer space? Does life exists on other planets in the form of aliens, and might they try to make contact with life on Earth? What do you think? And would you be frightened if you came across an alien from outer space?!?

These "Monsters"

Imagine a bat so large it darkens the sky.

Or a 25-foot-long shark with an enormous mouth. Do those animals frighten you? How about a spider that's bigger than your dinner plate?

Many people are terrified of **spiders**, **bugs**, **bats**, and **sharks**. It's true that they've had some bad press. Giant spiders attacked Harry Potter and his friends in *Harry Potter and the Prisoner of Azkaban*. The movie *Jaws* kept many people out of the ocean for fear of sharks. **Vampires** like Dracula are often shown turning into fierce vampire bats.

The truth, however, is nothing like the movies. Many animals earned the title of "monster" not because they are vicious but because they look terrifying. And looks can be deceiving.

The **grey-headed flying fox** of Australia is the world's largest bat. From wingtip to wingtip it is about a meter wide. It weighs over two pounds. It's so huge that it's actually called a "megabat." When it flies, it looks like a winged fox. These enormous and frightening animals, however, eat nothing but pollen, nectar, and fruit. Because they look so menacing, flying foxes have become the victims of human hunters. Today, they are considered an endangered species.

Basking sharks are the second-largest fish in the world. With their enormous mouths, they look like something out of a nightmare. But unlike their ferocious cousin the **great white shark**, basking sharks are harmless. Basking sharks have no

Need Your Help

by Lisa Jo Rudy

teeth at all – because they are filter feeders. They eat tiny sea creatures called plankton. Basking sharks are slow-moving and can even be playful. Unfortunately, they are also good to eat, so they are hunted around the world. As a result, they are in danger of extinction.

The **tree lobster** is an insect — but it's as large as a man's hand. It is also so rare that it was thought to be extinct. Then, in 2001, tree lobsters were rediscovered on Lord Howe Island near Australia. Though they look vicious, these stick bugs are harmless. With help from human scientists, they are beginning to come back from near-extinction.

Huge, **hairy tarantulas** are giant spiders. Some, like the goliath birdeater, can grow to be a foot wide. Tarantulas look like monsters. But few tarantulas bite at all, and some tarantulas are so gentle that they are kept as pets! Many types of tarantulas, especially those that live in the tropical rainforest, are endangered. As trees are cut and burned for farms, tarantulas lose their homes.

Now that you know a little more about our planet's "monsters," you may not be so frightened of bats, spiders, or sharks. In fact, you may actually want to help these creatures to survive. If so, think about getting involved with a conservation group in your area. Or join up with an international group like the World Wildlife Federation, and help save a monster or two!

FACE YOUR FEARS

by Lisa Jo Rudy

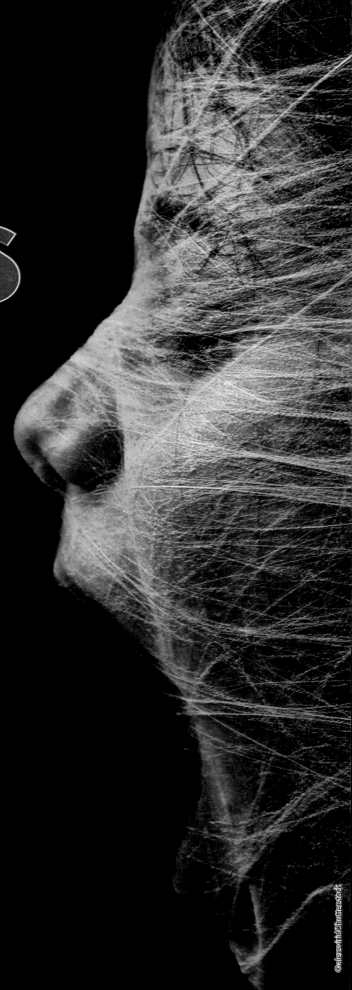

Do you feel shaky before a big exam? Nervous about speaking in front of your class? Are you sometimes scared of the dark or haunted by a horror film? If you answer "yes" to any of these questions, relax. You're not alone. Everyone — adults and kids alike — feels fear and anxiety.

If fear and anxiety are part of your life, you're perfectly normal. But that doesn't make the experience pleasant. And if fear and anxiety get in the way of enjoying or succeeding in life, you need some skills to manage them.

Are fear and anxiety problems for you? Answer these questions to help you decide. If you answer "yes" to more than one or two, take a look at the stress busters in the Tips for Coping the end of the article.

Ask Yourself:

Do I ever decide not to do something I'd probably enjoy because I'm so anxious about it?

Do I ever choose not to speak up in class because I'm afraid of what might happen next?

Do I ever find it hard to sleep because I'm thinking about a frightening TV show or movie?

Do I ever do badly on a test NOT because I don't know the answers but because I'm so anxious about taking the test?

Do I ever tell myself "I can't do this" even when I have the skills I need to succeed?

Do I ever think "I'm the only one in the world who has these bad feelings?"

If you're like most kids, chances are that you answered "yes" to at least a couple of these questions. If you're like many kids, you answered "yes" to three or more. That's because – let's face it – life is stressful. Kids cope with long school days, lots of tests, and high expectations from teachers, parents, and coaches.

Tips for Coping:

Relax. Simple relaxation methods can really make a difference, especially when you're about to take on a stressful activity like a test or public speaking. Try taking a few deep breaths, breathing in with your mouth and out through your nose. Now, close your eyes. Continuing to breathe deeply, imagine yourself somewhere calm and beautiful, anywhere that makes you happy. When you open your eyes, you'll feel a little calmer and readier to take on a challenge.

Sleep (and cut down on creepy TV). Sleep is very important, and people who get too little sleep are more likely to feel out of control. To get more sleep, you may need to cut down on TV (especially scary shows, which can cause nightmares or make it hard to fall asleep). You may also need to get to bed a little earlier, especially on weeknights.

Tell yourself what you need to hear. Many people spend most of the day giving themselves negative messages. "I can't." "I don't have the intelligence/strength/popularity to succeed." These messages are part of the problem. Instead, give yourself positive messages. "I look great." "I studied, and I'll get an A." Positive messages (called affirmations) make a difference.

You can't get rid of anxiety and fear. They're just part of life. But you can learn to live — and thrive — with your feelings.

Are **You** Afraid **of** Riddles?

Some people have a fear of failure – so they don't even try to solve riddles. But if you read all the articles in this magazine, you'll have no trouble at all. If you need a hint, take a look at the pictures to find clues.

1 At close of day you fear the **park**

Because you are afraid of the ___.

2 You love dogs and cuddle **cats**—

And yet you are afraid of ___.

3 An elevator never **bites,**

But it's scary when you fear great ___.

4 This animal can leave a **mark,**

So many fear the lethal ___.

5 In flower beds you gasp and **freeze**

Because you are afraid of ___.

4. SHARK 5. BEES

1. DARK 2. RATS 3. HEIGHTS

Animal Intelligence

Ivan the Gorilla ✳ Pigeons ✳ Whales and Dolphins ✳ Dogs ✳ Cephalopods

Cleanup Time!

Sit! Shake! Roll Over! Fetch! Lie Down! Stay!

It's fun to teach your dog tricks. With time, patience, and *lots of treats*, your pooch can learn these commands and more. Here are a few important rules to remember.

CONNECT! Training is easier if you and your dog have a strong bond. When there is a bond, your dog will listen to you when you talk and will try to please you.

START SMALL. Begin with an easy trick, like "Sit!" Build up to more difficult tricks gradually.

GIVE LOTS OF REWARDS. When your dog is learning a new trick, be sure to reward him with praise and a treat whenever he does what you ask. Reward the correct behavior as quickly as possible—even if your dog has done it by mistake.

PIECE IT TOGETHER. Break down longer tricks into small chunks that your dog can learn one step at a time. When the first step is mastered, add a second, and so on.

You can use the same basic method to teach your dog any new trick. Your dog will be rolling over and shaking hands in no time at all.

©Jeff Thrower/Shutterstock

18

Little kids learn to pick up after themselves, so why not your pup?

Once your dog has learned the basic commands, you can move on to something more complicated. Here's a step-by-step guide to teaching your dog one of the most useful tricks of all: picking up his toys!

(Note: it is easier to teach this trick if your dog already knows the commands "Fetch!" and "Let go!")

1. Sit on the floor next to your dog's toy box or basket. Take a toy and throw it across the room. When your dog chases it, hold a treat over the basket and call him back. Say, "Clean up!" or "Basket!" or whatever command name you choose.

2. Holding the treat directly over the basket, tell your dog to let go. When the toy falls in the basket, give your dog the treat and lots of praise!

   Note: If your dog drops the toy before he reaches the basket, hide the treat and tell your dog to go back and fetch. Don't give the treat until he brings the toy right to the basket. Be patient: it may take your dog some time to get the hang of this.

3. Repeat many times, gradually moving the toy basket away from you. At first you can hold the treat over the basket by holding out your arm. Eventually you can just point to the basket.

4. In the beginning, doggie gets a treat each time he puts a toy in the basket. Gradually build up until he just gets one reward after he has picked up all his toys. Good dog!

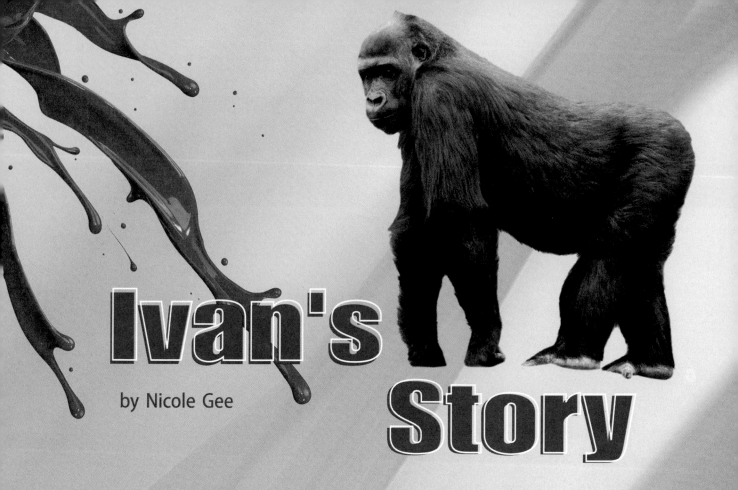

Ivan's Story

by Nicole Gee

Ivan acted a lot like an ordinary kid. He loved to sleep late. He liked to wear hats. He would drink out of cups. He played with a stuffed animal. His favorite activity was painting, and his favorite color was red. Ivan *especially* didn't like cold, rainy days.

Ivan was a gorilla — a silverback gorilla.

Ivan and his twin sister were born in the Democratic Republic of the Congo in Africa. When they were babies, they were captured and sold to a department store in Tacoma, Washington. After they arrived in the U.S., Ivan's sister died.

Ivan spent his first few years living as a pet owned by the family of the department store manager. He learned to watch television and eat at the family table.

When Ivan grew too large to keep as a pet, he was moved to a small glass-enclosed cage in the shopping mall where the department store was located. Ivan would live there by himself for 27 years, on display for the customers.

During this time Ivan learned to finger paint. He signed his paintings with his thumbprints. Ivan was a popular attraction at the mall.

Eventually, people began to clamor that it wasn't right to keep this intelligent and social animal confined in such an isolated and tiny cell.

After animal rights activists called for an end to Ivan's isolated captivity, he was moved to the gorilla exhibit at Zoo Atlanta. For the first time in decades, Ivan walked outdoors.

Ivan especially loved sunny days. He enjoyed being outside with the trees, grass, and fresh air. But when it would rain, Ivan would either stay inside or use burlap bags to cover his feet. He did not like getting wet!

Ivan had the companionship of not only other apes, but also the primate keepers at the zoo. In fact, he formed a very close bond with his keeper, Jodi Carrigan.

Ivan could make his feelings known to Jodi and his other keepers. Jodi said that Ivan's eyes were very expressive. He was also very determined about demanding what he wanted. He would knock noisily until one of the keepers noticed. Ivan made his voice heard!

Ivan also had his silly moments. One time he wanted to scare Jodi, so he hid in a big box. Jodi couldn't find him and kept calling his name. Imagine Jodi's astonishment when he jumped out of the box and surprised her!

Ivan continued to be an avid painter, but now he used a brush. His keepers would line up his paint cans, he would point to which can he wanted to use, and his keepers would then pour out the paint and hand him a brush. When he finished painting, he would return the brush to his keepers.

Ivan lived at the Zoo Atlanta for 18 years. When he died at the age of 50, he was mourned by many people. To those who knew and visited him, Ivan was special. He had an intelligent mind, a sweet spirit, and a strong personality. Ivan had made the most of his unusual life.

Homing Pigeons

Finding Their Way Home

Homing pigeons are ordinary-looking birds with an extraordinary ability: they can quickly and reliably find their way home, even when released from as far as 1,000 miles away. They fly home even when starting out from places they have never been before. They travel at up to 60 miles per hour, fly sometimes for as long as 15 hours without stopping, and end up back at their very own cozy pigeon loft—a microscopic dot on a huge map. Neat trick!

Humans have been making use of the homing pigeon's natural talent for thousands of years. As long as 3,000 years ago, people began using pigeons to carry messages. (A homing pigeon carrying a message is called a carrier pigeon.) The Ancient Greeks, for example, used carrier pigeons to tell people in surrounding cities of Olympic victories. The Romans were the first of many to use pigeons to send information from the battlefront. During World War I and World War II, carrier pigeons were still being used to deliver coded messages. Pigeons have been used for a postal service, to ferry specimens between hospitals, and to send out stock-market reports.

Even today, when electronic communication has replaced pigeon-messengers, thousands of enthusiasts raise pigeons to race in homing competitions. It's a popular 4-H activity. Over the centuries, homing pigeons have been selectively bred to fly faster and get home over longer distances. Today's champion homers are like athletes: they're pampered with the best food and given plenty of exercise and practice. Races are monitored electronically, with a bird's tag clocking it in as it crosses the threshold back into its home loft.

That's All Very Interesting, But How Do They Do it?

How homing pigeons navigate is one of science's enduring mysteries. Scientists know they need the equivalent of both a compass and a map. A compass tells you which direction is north, south, east, and west. But it's of little use without a map, because a compass doesn't tell where you are relative to home. (If home is Boston, from Florida you go north, but from Canada you go south.) Likewise, knowing where you are on a map doesn't help if you can't tell which way you're headed.

Many scientists believe that homing pigeons use the earth's magnetic field as a compass. Strong evidence points to their using both the sun and the stars as well. But what do they use for a map? Scientists have studied the question for years. Here are three theories they've put forward.

Odor

SCIENTISTS IN ITALY DISCOVERED THAT if you deprive a pigeon of its sense of smell, it has difficulty finding its way home. They suggested that, from an early age, pigeons learn to recognize the smell profile of their home loft. They associate odors with wind direction and build up a "smell map" of the wider environment. This could allow them to navigate using smell. Other scientists are not so sure. How, they ask, could pigeons use smell to navigate when they are 100, 500, or 1,000 miles from home?

Magnetism

SOME SCIENTISTS BELIEVE THAT homing pigeons use the earth's magnetic field as both compass AND map. The earth's magnetic field is not the same all over. As it interacts with magnetic material in the earth's crust, it dips, rises, and twists. The magnetic field ends up having a unique shape that can be used like a map. Scientists have shown evidence that pigeons search for the magnetic contour line that passes through their loft and follow it home.

The problem is, experiments have shown that pigeons can find their way home even if you purposefully disrupt their ability to use the earth's magnetic field. Hmmm. Looks like we need another theory!

Infrasound

YOU'VE PROBABLY NEVER HEARD of infrasound—and you certainly haven't ever *heard* it. Humans can't hear infrasound because the frequency is too low, but homing pigeons can. Infrasound is like the low, quiet rumble of the earth. Every spot on earth has its own infrasound signature that travels for thousands of miles. The evidence suggests that homing pigeons use the infrasonic signature of their loft to navigate home. This theory is the most promising yet—but it still needs to be confirmed.

Some scientists suggest homing pigeons use all of these means of navigation, and maybe more. Just as we use a combination of ways to get from place to place (GPS, maps, instructions, remembered landmarks), homing pigeons probably rely on a number of navigation methods.

Just because there's no longer any "pigeon post" doesn't mean homing pigeons aren't still helpful to us. Studying how they navigate can give us useful ideas. For example, currently we rely on satellites to run our GPS systems. But what if satellites weren't available? Perhaps developing a navigational system based on infrasound would be a good idea, at least as a back up. Now, if only we could get homing pigeons to tell us exactly how that works. . . .

What Did That Whale Just Say?

by Lisa Jo Rudy

Whales and dolphins are some of the smartest animals on the planet. Both whales and dolphins are mammals—like humans, dogs, and elephants. And, like humans, dogs, and elephants, whales and dolphins use sounds and motions to communicate with one another. Scientists are working hard to figure out how these animals communicate. Someday, people may be able to have a conversation with whales or dolphins!

How Whales Talk

Most whales communicate to identify themselves, warn other whales about dangers, and try to find a mate. Whales also may "talk" about their feelings to one another. Here are some of the ways they communicate:

♦ Chirps and whistles (especially baleen whales)

♦ Moaning sounds

♦ Mating songs (humpback whales)

♦ Slapping flippers together

♦ Blowing water in certain ways

Dolphin Communication

Dolphins have very close friends and family, but they also swim in pods, or herds. They use sounds, motions, and physical touch to communicate.

Some scientists believe that every dolphin has its own special whistle. This whistle identifies each dolphin just as a name identifies each human. When they are excited, dolphins call their own "name" loudly, over and over again—much as a human being might call for help. They can also call other dolphins' names to get their attention.

Researchers have watched dolphins carefully to figure out just what their movements mean. They know that calves often stay close to their mothers, which seems to be a sign of love. Dolphins may also get rough with one another when competing for a mate. When dolphins follow boats and chirp to humans, they may be showing curiosity. But no one really knows for sure what dolphins mean when they wag their heads from side to side, roll their eyes, or roll over.

We imagine dolphins' conversations are very interesting. But until we break the code, we can only guess what they're chatting about.

How Smart Is Your Dog?

Border Collie

Poodle

Which dogs are the smartest? Here are ten breeds of dogs that are really smart.

Plenty of people think their dogs are smart. But are they right? According to researchers, the answer is "yes." In fact, most dogs are as smart as a human two-year-old. Even not-so-smart dogs can recognize about 165 human words, and bright dogs understand about 250. One particularly intelligent dog named Chaser has learned the names of more than 1,000 different toys, and can find the right toy when asked.

While not all dogs can listen to and understand a thousand words, most dogs are very good at watching and understanding our movements. When we point, they follow our fingers. When we look unhappy, they work hard to comfort us.

Because dogs are so good at communicating with people, they are sometimes called "man's best friend." In addition to being friends, however, dogs have long been trained to work with people.

German Shepherd

Golden Retriever

Australian
Cattle Dog

What does it take to be a working dog? To start with, a working dog must be able to follow instructions – sitting, standing, and responding when they hear a particular word or hand movement. But to be a really reliable working dog, they must also learn something called "intelligent disobedience." When a dog is intelligently disobedient, it will follow human instructions unless the instructions will lead the dog or the human into danger.

Intelligent disobedience is especially important for dogs that are trained to guide people who are blind or deaf. Of course, the dog must obey their owner's commands. But what if their owner isn't aware that a car is coming when they are about to cross the street? A trained guide dog will refuse to move if he sees danger coming.

In addition to guiding people with disabilities, dogs are trained for many different jobs. They may work with therapists to help people feel a sense of companionship, comfort, or safety. They may guard livestock such as sheep or goats.

While dogs are smart enough to be trained, it's their connection to people that make them special to us.

Rottweiler

Papillon

Labrador
Retriever

Doberman
Pinscher

Shetland
Sheepdog

Cephalopods
Masters of Camouflage

Many animals can hide in plain sight, but none can match the camouflage skills of the cephalopods. The squid, octopus, and cuttlefish have the ability to change not just the color and pattern of their skin, but its texture as well. All of that in the blink of an eye!

Cephalopods are mollusks, like clams and mussels, but they lack the hard outer covers that help keep their shellfish cousins safe. Instead, many cephalopods have perfected the art of camouflage. They can change the color and pattern on their skin in less than a second—far faster than any other creature. And cephalopods can change their skin texture as well.

An octopus or cuttlefish controls muscles that can change the surface of its skin, enabling it to match the texture of rock, coral, or kelp, for example. Then, when it imitates the shape of the object with its soft, flexible body, it creates a nearly perfect copy.

Intelligent Invertebrates

Cephalopods — the octopus, squid, and cuttlefish — are the most intelligent of the invertebrates. Their brain to body ratio is the highest of any invertebrate. Scientists say that cephalopods can learn new things, remember information, and solve problems.

Cephalopods are predators, and one way they developed their intelligence was through the need to locate and catch their prey. Octopi, for example, have figured out how to steal lobsters from lobster traps. Some octopi have even climbed into fishing boats to capture crabs.

Cephalopods can manipulate objects and use them as tools. Octopi have been observed picking up and carrying shells and using them to create shelter. While squid, like other cephalopods, can change skin color and pattern for camouflage, they also apparently use these changes to communicate with other squid.

What's even more amazing is that cephalopods can successfully imitate colors around them despite the fact that they themselves are colorblind. Scientists are not exactly sure what mechanism they use to assess and match the color shades and patterns in their surroundings—something they can do even in the pitch dark. Cuttlefish continue to camouflage themselves all night long: their skin never sleeps.

How does the color display in a cephalopod's skin work? In a layer of cells just below the surface of the skin there are millions of cells with little pigment sacs. The muscles around the pigment sacs stretch and squeeze, changing the animal's color shades and patterns. Cephalopods may become invisible—or, in different circumstances, to stand out. Certain species of cuttlefish use flashing color patterns to hypnotize their prey. Bright color patterns in other cephalopod species warn potential predators that what they are about to eat is poisonous!

What Are the Animals Saying?

Each of these animals is saying something—but what message are they sending? Match the description of body language with the animal.

crouches to show
it wants to play

dances to show it
found nectar

rubs noses to
show friendship

lies on back to
show it feels safe

puts ears forward
to show curiosity

flicks tail to show
danger is near

Dealing with

DISASTER

10 Tips to Stay

It's no fun to think about, but it's important to know what to do if there's a fire at your home. Here are ten tips that can help you stay safe.

1 Get out fast

☞ During a fire, getting out as quickly as possible is the most important thing.

2 Call 911 only when you are safe

☞ Don't stay in the house to call 911. You can find a way to call once you are safely outside.

3 You first, pets later

☞ Do not stay inside or go back inside to look for or chase a pet. When the firefighters arrive, you can tell them about pets that are still inside.

4 Get under the smoke

☞ Breathing in smoke from a fire is very dangerous and should be avoided as much as possible. Because smoke rises, you can steer clear of the worst by staying low. If you see smoke, get as low to the floor as you can and crawl out to safety.

5 Before you open that door . . .

If you are in a room with no fire, **don't open the door if:**

☞ there's smoke or heat coming under the door;

☞ the door is hot;

☞ the doorknob is hot or very warm.

SAFE IN A FIRE

6 If the way out is blocked

☞ If smoke or fire is blocking your way, yell for help. Call 911 if you have a phone with you.

☞ Stay where you can easily be seen and found. Never hide in a closet or under a bed.

☞ If there is a window that you can't use to escape, open it and stand in front of it.

7 Stop the smoke

☞ If you cannot escape, keep smoke out of the room by blocking cracks around the door. Use wet towels or cloth, if possible.

8 Stop, drop, and roll

☞ If something you are wearing catches fire, don't panic, and don't run! Drop to the ground, cover your face with your hands, and roll. This will put out the flames.

9 Memorize your escape route

☞ Memorize the fastest escape routes from each room so you can quickly get out of the house, even if it is smoky or dark.

☞ Plan a second escape route in case the best way out is blocked by fire or smoke. Remember first-floor windows are also possible exits.

10 Plan and practice with your family

☞ Decide on a meeting point outside, such as a neighbor's porch or anywhere else nearby.

☞ Have an annual family fire drill to practice using your planned escape routes.

BEWARE
OF YOUR FRIENDLY NEIGHBORHOOD VOLCANO

by Lisa Jo Rudy

Mount Saint Helens, Washington

On Sunday, May 18, 1980, the ground near Mount Saint Helens volcano in Washington began to shake. The rocks on the north face of the mountain slid away, forming the biggest landslide ever recorded. What happened next had not happened for 75 years. The volcano exploded! Lava and rock flew from its mouth. The molten mess poured down the mountain toward beautiful Spirit Lake.

By the time Mount Saint Helens had stopped erupting, 57 people were dead. A lake had been buried. Thousands of wild animals had died.

What happened in Washington could happen again today. In fact, there are 169 volcanoes in the United States. Of these, 18 are considered to be a "very high threat." This means that there is a real possibility that more volcanoes will errupt within the next ten to twenty years. Many of these active volcanoes are in Hawaii and Alaska. Others are on the west coast of the United States, in Oregon, Washington, and California.

Some of the "very high threat" volcanoes on the west coast have not erupted for thousands of years. These pictured volcanoes, however, have all erupted much more recently.

Mount Ranier last erupted in 1895. However, it could cause landslides with even a small eruption. Lassen Peak erupted in 1915, spreading volcanic ash for 200 miles. Mount Hood's last large eruption was around 1800, and Mount Baker had its last eruption in 1880, but scientists expect it to erupt again.

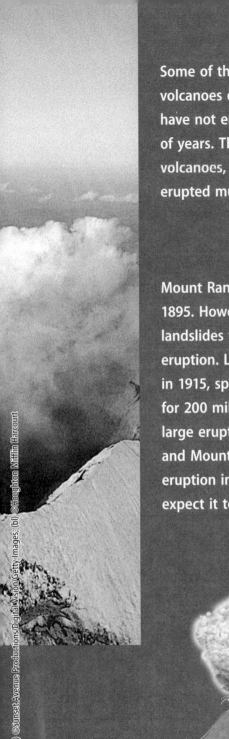

Mount Rainer, Washington

Lassen Peak , California

Mount Hood , Oregon

Mount Baker , Washington

CITIES

by Nancy Brookes Sayres

Chicago and **S**an **F**rancisco were nearly destroyed by disasters. But the cities were rebuilt to be safer in the future.

IN RUIN

THE CHICAGO FIRE OF 1871

On the night of October 8, 1871, a fire started in Chicago. Fire fighters fought hard, but the blaze spread rapidly. There had been little rain in the city for months, and the night was very windy.

The fire destroyed many wooden buildings, roads, and sidewalks. It burned down factories and the courthouse. Finally, it took down the waterworks, and fire fighters had no water for fighting the fire.

Late on October 9, it began to rain. Little by little, the fire went out. When it finally ended, much of Chicago was in ruin. Three hundred people had died, and 100,000 people were homeless. The people of Chicago rebuilt their city, with buildings that were less likely to burn. In addition, they developed one of the best fire-fighting forces in the country.

THE SAN FRANCISCO
EARTHQUAKE OF 1906

San Francisco has had several earthquakes, but the one that caused the most damage was in 1906. This earthquake caused more deaths than any other natural disaster in the history of California.

San Francisco and the surrounding area sit on the San Andreas fault. A *fault* is a crack in the surface of the Earth where huge plates meet. The plates shift, causing the ground to shake or even split open. Since San Francisco is on a fault, it is likely to have earthquakes.

On April 18, 1906, at 5:13 a.m., San Francisco's deadliest earthquake struck. It started with a tremor, or shaking, which led to fires. Then the violently moving earth broke the city water pipes. Without water, fire fighters could not fight the fire, and it spread across the city.

The fire burned for days. In the end, over 3,000 people died. Nearly 28,000 buildings were destroyed. More than a quarter of a million people were left without homes.

The people of San Francisco quickly began to rebuild their city. Before 1906, no one had given much thought about building a city that could withstand earthquakes. After 1906, however, engineers began working on earthquake-proofing buildings and water systems. Today, San Francisco is relatively safe, although another major earthquake is always possible.

41

What's So Great About Shocking Movies?

by Helen Warren

Everyone loves disaster and monster movies. Maybe it's fun to see how people can survive even the worst catastrophe. Maybe it's nice to know that people are braver than they think they are. Or perhaps we just enjoy being scared!

There are many different kinds of disaster movies. They all, however, are built around a catastrophic event. There are lots of special effects and explosions. Some people show their cowardly side by shoving others away and saving themselves. Others discover that they are braver than they ever thought possible.

One of the very first disaster movies came out in 1912. It was called *Saved from the Titanic*, and it told the story of a woman who had survived the famous ship wreck just months before.

Another disaster movie based on a true event was *In Old Chicago*, which was about the 1871 fire. Appearing in the 1930s, it was the most expensive movie ever made at the time—because of its special effects.

(b) ©Trueboy/Shutterstock

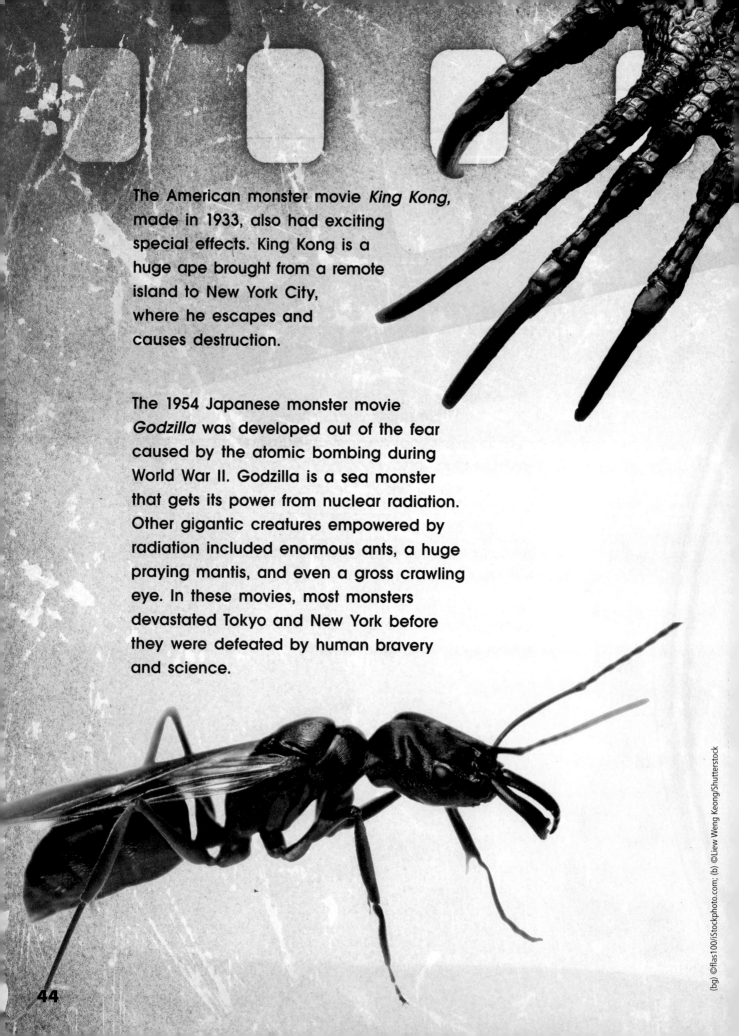

The American monster movie *King Kong*, made in 1933, also had exciting special effects. King Kong is a huge ape brought from a remote island to New York City, where he escapes and causes destruction.

The 1954 Japanese monster movie *Godzilla* was developed out of the fear caused by the atomic bombing during World War II. Godzilla is a sea monster that gets its power from nuclear radiation. Other gigantic creatures empowered by radiation included enormous ants, a huge praying mantis, and even a gross crawling eye. In these movies, most monsters devastated Tokyo and New York before they were defeated by human bravery and science.

In the 1970s, everyone was going to disaster movies. There were disasters in skyscrapers (*Towering Inferno*), disasters in airplanes (*Airport*) and disasters in boats (*The Poseidon Adventure*). While these movies are scary, special effects in more recent films make the disaster seem almost real. The movie *Twister* puts viewers into the middle of a realistic tornado. The movies *Volcano* and *Dante's Peak* seem to radiate the heat of molten lava.

What so great about shocking movies? Disaster and monster movies are a good way for us to enjoy the excitement of catastrophes without any of the danger!

Planning for an Emergency

We all hope disaster will never strike our homes or neighborhoods. Even so, it's better to be prepared. Sit down with your parents and make a family emergency plan. Tailor your plan according to where you live. For example, in California, you'll want to prepare for a possible earthquake.

Here are some basic components your family emergency plan should include, no matter where you live.

Choose a Meeting Place

Agree on two family meeting places, one near your home, and one outside your neighborhood in case you have to evacuate the area. Everyone in the family should plan to gather at the meeting point as quickly as possible.

Map out an Exit

Make sure everyone in the family knows the quickest way to get out of the house from every room. Have a back-up escape route planned in case a path is blocked.

Plan to Stay in Touch

When disaster strikes, you'll need to be in touch with family members.

Choose one person to be your family's emergency contact. Instead of each family member trying to contact the others, everyone reports in to the emergency contact and is updated about other family members. Be sure to choose someone out of your area. In a disaster, phone lines can be down, slow, or jammed. Having an emergency contact far enough away increases the likelihood of smooth communication.

Prepare an Emergency Kit

Make up one emergency kit for your house and one for each car in the family. Kits should contain a battery-powered radio, a flashlight with extra batteries, snacks, and plenty of water. Also include a first-aid kit, blankets, clothes, and sturdy shoes, if possible.

Practice and Repeat

Make your family emergency planning meeting a yearly event. You can practice quickly leaving the house. You can update contact information, refresh emergency-kit supplies, and make sure everyone remembers the designated meeting points and the contact person. In an emergency, preparation, practice, and planning can really pay off.

Do You Know Your Natural Disasters?

There are many different kinds of natural disasters (disasters caused by the natural world). Can you name them all? Match the pictures to the names and definitions!

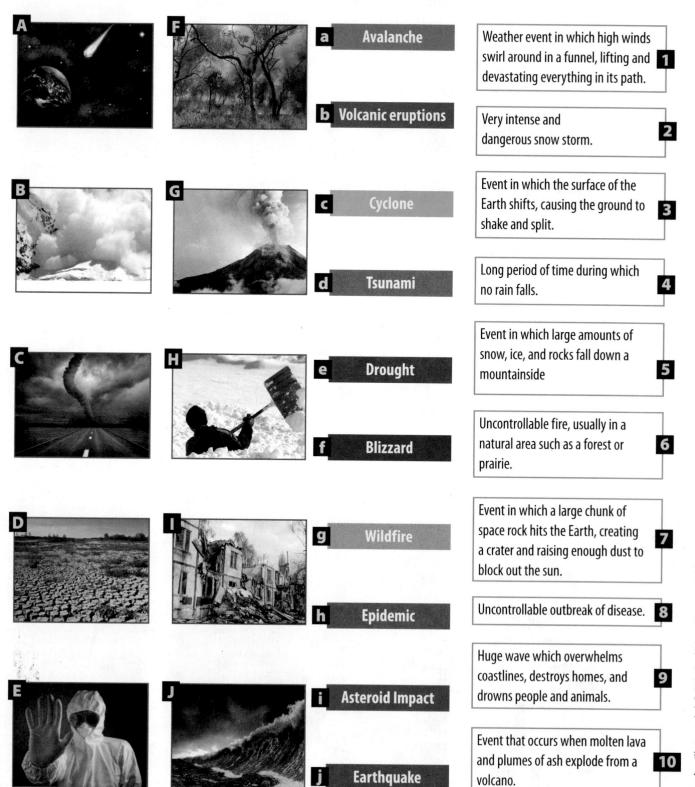

a Avalanche

b Volcanic eruptions

c Cyclone

d Tsunami

e Drought

f Blizzard

g Wildfire

h Epidemic

i Asteroid Impact

j Earthquake

1 Weather event in which high winds swirl around in a funnel, lifting and devastating everything in its path.

2 Very intense and dangerous snow storm.

3 Event in which the surface of the Earth shifts, causing the ground to shake and split.

4 Long period of time during which no rain falls.

5 Event in which large amounts of snow, ice, and rocks fall down a mountainside

6 Uncontrollable fire, usually in a natural area such as a forest or prairie.

7 Event in which a large chunk of space rock hits the Earth, creating a crater and raising enough dust to block out the sun.

8 Uncontrollable outbreak of disease.

9 Huge wave which overwhelms coastlines, destroys homes, and drowns people and animals.

10 Event that occurs when molten lava and plumes of ash explode from a volcano.

Answers: 1 C c; 2 H f; 3 I j; 4 D e; 5 B a; 6 F g; 7 A i; 8 E h; 9 J d; 10 G b

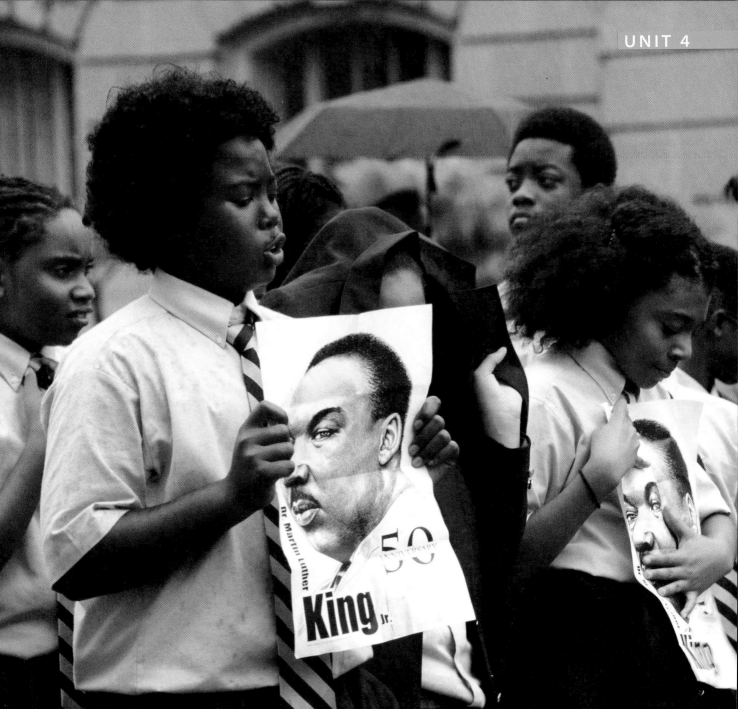

MAKING YOUR VOICE HEARD

Agatha Christie * Public Speaking * Vote! * Vlogs * James Earl Jones

Hercule Poirot and Miss Marple: The Voice of Agatha Christie

by Jess R. Logan

MR. HERCULE POIROT AND MISS JANE MARPLE are two of England's most beloved literary characters. Poirot and Marple are detectives created by Agatha Christie, who is one othe the best-selling novelists in the world. Agatha Christie found her voice as a writer with these two characters, and she wrote more than sixty mystery novels, many with these detectives.

Agatha was born in 1890 in England. She had a happy childhood. She loved to read, and adored her pets. Agatha played the piano and the mandolin, and once performed in a musical play with her friends. Years later, as an adult, she wrote plays as well as novels.

During World War I, Agatha worked in a pharmacy in London and volunteered to help wounded soldiers. She got the idea for Hercule Poirot when she saw many refugees in England after Germany invaded Belgium. Poirot was a former Belgian police officer living in England. He had a large mustache, an egg-shaped head, and a very big ego.

In 1920, Christie published her first book, *The Mysterious Affair at Styles*, featuring the Belgian detective Hercule Poirot. Many readers were riveted by Christie's detailed descriptions of Poirot's careful observations and clever deduction, or inference, skills. These readers were also fascinated by a soon-to-be-famous Christie style element: the final denouement. This is the conclusion of the novel when the main character reveals the solution to the mystery.

After the war ended, Christie began writing more novels. Her murder mysteries and thrillers featured the logical, perceptive, and beloved Hercule Poirot. She also introduced a new character, the intelligent and shrewd Miss Jane Marple, as a detective. Christie based Miss Marple on her grandmother. She later said that both her grandmother and Miss Marple always expected the worst and were often right.

The Orient Express

In 1934 Agatha traveled on the Orient Express, a luxury train running between Paris, France, and Istanbul, Turkey. She based her novel *Murder on the Orient Express* on this experience.

Christie set many of her novels in places she visited on her travels. When she spent time in the Middle East with her husband, Max Mallowan, an archaeologist, she wrote a historical detective novel, *Death Comes as the End*, which took place in Thebes in 2000 BCE. Christie set modern novels in the Middle East as well, including *Death on the Nile* and *Murder in Mesopotamia*. But many of her books took place in England.

Over the years, Agatha grew tired of her character Hercule Poirot. She wanted to kill him off in a book, but resisted because she knew her fans loved to read about him. However, she stayed fond of her detective, Miss Marple. Although these two characters are the primary voices of Agatha Christie, she never put them in a novel together. She thought Poirot would not accept working with an elderly lady like Miss Marple.

Agatha Christie

Agatha Christie's Legacy

* Over a billion copies of Agatha Christie's books have been sold in English.

* Agatha Christie's books have translated into over 100 languages.

* Agatha Christie's books are only outsold by Shakespeare's works and the Bible.

* Her play *The Mousetrap* is the longest-running show in the history of theater.

Facts about Agatha Christie

* Christie wrote six romance novels under the name of Mary Westmacott.

* Christie considered *The Murder of Roger Ackroyd* and *Endless Night* to be two of her favorite novels.

* Christie received the Commander of the Order of the British Empire in 1971. The Order of the British Empire rewards those who have provided valuable service to the United Kingdom and its people.

Did You Know?

* Hercule Poirot and Miss Marple aren't Christie's only fictional detectives. Christie's detectives also include Harley Quin, Parker Pyne, Ariadne Oliver, and Tommy and Tuppence.

* Tommy and Tuppence are the only Christie characters to age with each book.

Overcoming the Fear of Public Speaking

by Casey Sullivan

Public speaking is one of most people's greatest fears. In fact, along with spiders and heights, public speaking is one of the most common phobias. The idea of speaking in front of a crowd, whether giving a speech in front of classmates, or a presentation at work, can cause many people's hands to sweat, voice to tremble, and stomach to turn. Some people will go to great lengths to avoid speaking in public. They'll skip a class that requires them to present, or take a back seat at work while someone more outgoing takes the lead. There's no need to let anxiety get in your way, however. With practice, anyone can overcome the fear of public speaking. Here are some simple tips to help.

Know your stuff. The more you've mastered the material you're presenting, the more confident you'll be. If you're afraid of messing up a speech on the world's greatest leaders, or a debate over nuclear power, knowing the issue well will make you feel ready to explain it to others. The more knowledge you have, the less likely you'll be to make a mistake and get off track.

Treat your audience as your friend. You'll almost never have an audience that wants you to fail. Remember, the audience isn't there to judge you. They're there to learn. If you are intimidated speaking in front of strangers, imagine that you're speaking to your best friend or a family member instead.

Practice, practice, practice!
The more you practice public speaking, the more comfortable you will be. If you have a presentation to give, run through it from start to finish several times beforehand.

Lighten Up. It's no fun to embarrass yourself or do less than a perfect job, but remember, even your worst failure won't be that bad. After all, it's just public speaking. If you can take some of the pressure off yourself and your own expectations, you're less likely to suffer from anxiety.

Take a breath and don't be afraid of silence. Taking two deep, slow breaths before speaking can help calm you down. If you're speaking in public and you've made a mistake—maybe you've lost track of where you are or you've begun rambling—feel free to pause for a second, take a deep breath and refocus.

Finally, if all else fails, you can always take this age-old advice: imagine your audience in their underwear.

Why It's Important to Vote

by Vivian Chang

Who is in charge of your government? Yes, politicians make choices about what laws to pass, the mayor decides how to spend the town's money, and government officials decide how to administer programs. But in a democracy, all of their power comes from you. It is your voice and your vote that helps determine how your country is run. There are a lot of ways you can impact your government, but the most fundamental is through voting.

Voting is a main way we influence our government. It's how we decide who is going to lead us and what they should do. However, in many presidential elections, barely half the people who could vote actually cast a ballot. That's a shame, since the person who wins an election is chosen only by those who vote in it. When you vote, the government doesn't know who you voted for.

Of course, you can't vote in elections until you turn 18, but you can become an informed citizen now. You can vote in elections in your school. If students run for class offices or for student council, you can learn about candidates, so you know who you want to vote for. You can also learn about issues other students care about and run for office yourself! Being involved in school elections can help you prepare to be an informed voter when you grow up.

Another way to prepare to be a responsible voter is to study issues you care about. Many students are concerned about the environment. Find out what is happening that affects the environment in your area. Are there streams that are contaminated? Is there a problem with air pollution? You can learn about these matters by reading your community newspaper or checking local websites. There may be organizations that are already involved in dealing with these issues, and you could join and help out.

You can be involved in any issue. Do you think your school needs more art and music classes? Do you think your city needs more parks? Do you think your town should put in bike lanes? You can learn about the issue, work with other people, and make your voice heard, even before you are old enough to vote.

And if you are already an informed citizen, when you are 18 and can vote, you will know what and who you want to vote for. Then you can influence your government even more!

YOUR VLOG, YOUR VOICE

by Esme Ramos

Have you ever wanted to start a vlog, or an online video blog? If so, you most likely have watched some vlogs. You also might know classmates or friends who have started vlogs.

Much like blogs, vlogs show your personality. But instead of writing and publishing blog posts, you film videos of yourself and post them online. When you publish blog posts, you are sharing content so that your readers can respond to your written voice. Similarly, when you film vlogs, you're talking to your audience. But instead of readers, your audience will be the viewers who will watch your vlogs. These viewers will respond to your spoken voice.

Like a blog post, a vlog has a topic. When you vlog, you tell your viewers how you feel about something. You may film videos about what you do every day. You can give reviews about your favorite books. You may tell jokes or record yourself speaking a comedy routine. Do you have a special talent? You can show

tutorials, or step-by-step instructions, for activities such as do-it-yourself crafting or cooking. Vlogs are a way of making your voice heard.

But how, exactly, do you make a vlog? Instead of using your blog software and template to write your blog, your main tool will be a camera. You use this camera to film your video. However, much like for a written online blog, you then use computer software to edit your video. Video editing is an activity in which you review your video content thoughtfully and make changes based on what the vlog content needs. For instance, if you are showing a beauty tutorial, did you forget to explain any steps about using and applying different makeup tools?

Even though you are not actually interacting with your viewers when you film your vlog, remember that viewers will be watching after you finish and post it. This is why video editing is an important step. You decide which scenes belong in your video and which do not.

Editing takes much more time than you might think. You have to carefully consider many aspects of your vlog. You might decide you need to shoot another scene to improve the transition between scenes. You might want to delete a scene because it is confusing or if it is not necessary. Whatever you decide, editing your video is crucial for your viewers' understanding. You want to make sure that your videos are entertaining. You also want to make sure that you are speaking clearly. Check that you are speaking at a pace that is easy for your viewers to understand.

Vlogging is a fun but public activity, so be sure that online safety is a priority. Do not give out any personal information, such as your telephone number or your address. If your friends join you on your videos, tell them that they are being recorded. It is not ethical, or right, to record people without their permission.

Your personality is your voice—and the voice of your vlog. The success of your vlog depends on how you communicate to others. Viewers connect to vloggers' videos because they find something they can relate to. For example, vloggers might have the same sense of humor as viewers have. Vloggers might shop in some of the same stores that viewers like. Viewers might listen to the same kind of music that vloggers enjoy. Viewers might have the same kind of pet, such as a dog or a cat. Viewers get a sense of the vloggers' personalities. So make sure that your personality shines through loud and clear in your vlog!

Always be polite and respectful to others when you vlog. Have fun!

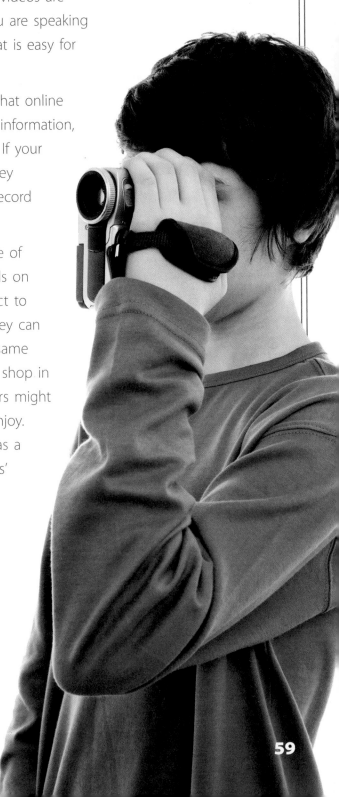

A Powerful Voice
with
Humble Beginnings

by Matt Silvestri

James Earl Jones' voice has struck fear in the hearts of creatures across a galaxy far, far away. It has also inspired a young lion prince to challenge his uncle and return peace to the animal kingdom. His voice is recognizable to moviegoers throughout the world. But it took most of his childhood for the actor to find the voice that would go on to star in two of the highest grossing movies of all time.

Jones was born in Mississippi in 1931 during the Depression. His father abandoned the family early in the boy's life. His grandparents adopted him and moved him from his home in Mississippi to their farm in Michigan when he was only five years old. The move was traumatic for a young boy who enjoyed the feel of the soil and the simplicity of life in rural Mississippi. He developed a stutter and nearly stopped talking.

Workers in Mississippi during the depression in the 1930s

Actor James Earl Jones with wife at the American Film Institute Life Achievement Award gala in Hollywood

According to Jones, he found talking difficult, so he just stopped. Instead, he focused on writing. Throughout his early education, the boy said very little in class. Even his oral exams were completed with a pen and paper. During this time, Jones developed into a talented poet. This skill earned the attention of a high school teacher.

After 8 years of silence Jones met a teacher named Donald Crouch, who took an interest in the quiet boy's poetry. He encouraged his pupil to share his poems every day in class, believing that forced public speaking would help the boy overcome the stutter. Crouch eventually succeeded after Jones wrote an especially good poem, "An Ode to Grapefruit." The teacher refused to believe the boy had written the poem himself unless he could speak it out loud. Jones stood in front of the class and read the poem without stuttering. He was surprised at his ability. He began to speak more.

Jones moved on to college and the military. During this time, he became interested in the theater. He was interested in the speaking that it involved. Because he had not spoken for so long, he had a great appreciation for its value. He switched his focus in college from pre-medicine to acting. Upon graduation, he did what he could to earn roles. Raised to be self-sufficient by his grandparents, Jones took jobs as a night janitor so that he could train and perform as an actor. Eventually he was cast in a play, but then a familiar difficulty presented itself again.

Jones had a part as a houseboy in a play about Franklin Roosevelt. He only had one line, but when he stepped onto the stage to deliver it, an old challenge reared its ugly head: he began to stutter. Nervous because he felt that the audience knew what was happening, he exited the stage. However, he never stuttered again on stage.

James Earl Jones works to control his stutter even today. His hard work has paid off. His is one of the most recognizable voices in movies. He starred as the voice of Darth Vader in the space epic *Star Wars*. He also delighted and inspired children as the voice of Mufasa, the father of Simba, in *The Lion King*. His performances as an actor have earned critical acclaim and awards. Today, well into his eighties, Jones continues to act in movies and on stage.

Mr. Jones' Career Highlights

Movies
- *The Great White Hope*
- *The Lion King*
- *Star Wars*
- *The Empire Strikes Back*
- *The Return of the Jedi*

Theater
- *Driving Miss Daisy*
- *The Great White Hope*
- *On Golden Pond*
- *You Can't Take It With You*
- *Othello*
- *Hamlet*
- *King Lear*
- *Of Mice and Men*

TV
- *Sesame Street*
- *Touched by an Angel*
- *The Simpsons* (3 episodes)

Honors and Awards
- 2012 Honorary Oscar
- 2002 Kennedy Center Honors
- 1975 Grammy Award for Best Spoken Word Album
- 1971 Most Promising Newcomer Golden Globe for *The Great White Hope*
- 2 Emmy Awards in 1991, as best actor (*Gabriel's Fire*) and best supporting actor (*Heat Wave*)
- 1969 Tony as best actor for *The Great White Hope*

How does that sound?

Let's get literal—when you make your voice heard . . . how does it sound? There are many adjectives to describe voices. Can you match each adjective to the right voice description?

1	It seems to come from the nose.
2	It sounds like speaker is about to cry.
3	It has a rough, low sound.
4	Sound is deep and comes from the back of the throat.
5	It doesn't have any ups or downs.
6	It's controlled and pleasant to hear.
7	It's loud and sounds rough.
8	It's high-pitched and unpleasant.
9	It's attractive and slightly mysterious.
10	It's clear, light, and pleasant.

nasal shrill modulated

brittle gruff silvery raucous

smokey guttural flat

Now, try speaking in each of these types of voices. How do you sound?

Decisions that Matter

✔ Reaching the Moon ✔ To Race or Not?
✔ A Park in the Desert ✔ Breaking
Barriers ✔ That Cat!

Kennedy

In the early 1960s, the United States was in the middle of a long struggle with its main rival, the Soviet Union. These two countries sought to show their superiority over each other. This conflict was called the "Cold War." The war was "cold" because there was never any direct combat between the two. Though they were enemies, the rival powers fought each other through a series of substitute struggles. They fought to see who could win the most allies. They fought to build the most weapons. Perhaps most memorably, they fought to demonstrate their power in space.

When John F. Kennedy became President in 1961, this "Space Race" was well underway. The Space Race was how people referred to the competition between the Soviets and the Americans to master space exploration. The Space Race led to many advancements, from the first Earth-made satellites being launched into space to unmanned missions sent to Mars.

and **Space**

by Casey Sullivan

As Kennedy began his presidency, the U.S. was running far behind in the competition for space. The race had begun in 1955, when the American government announced that it would send a satellite into space for the first time. The Soviet Union, wanting to show that it was just as capable as America, said that it too would be launching a satellite "in the near future." The race was on. Two years later, the Soviet Union gained the advantage by launching Sputnik 1, the first human-made object to reach space. No one had expected the Soviets to outpace the United States. In 1961, they surprised the world again. Yuri Gagarin, a Soviet cosmonaut, became the first person in space. In the race for the stars, the United States had twice lost to the Soviet Union. Many Americans were embarrassed, afraid, and shocked that the Soviets had consistently beat them to space.

Kennedy responded by investigating just how to beat the Soviet Union. He put his Vice President, Lyndon Johnson, in charge of researching how the U.S. could win the Space Race. There were two options available to NASA, the American space agency. One, the U.S. could attempt to build the first space station. Or two, NASA could send the first manned spaceship to the moon. Either choice would require billions of dollars in research, infrastructure, and investment. NASA's best engineers and physicists were put to work researching what would be needed for the U.S. to succeed. Would it even be possible to build a space station? To send someone to the moon? If it was, could they be certain that the Soviet Union wouldn't do it first?

Beating the Soviet Union in the Space Race would be scientifically difficult, but it wouldn't be easy politically either. Operating a space program costs billions of dollars a year. Many Americans wanted that money to be used here on Earth instead of getting us to space. Even Kennedy's science advisor, Jerome Wiesner, recommended against manned space exploration. He thought it would be too costly and dangerous. Kennedy himself had rejected a budget requested by NASA in 1961 because the space agency had asked for too much money.

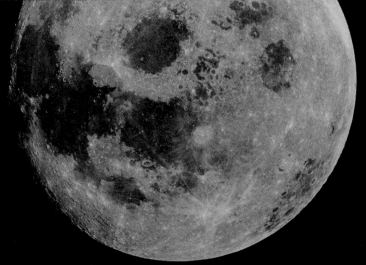

However, faced with the prospect of falling farther and farther behind the Soviet Union, Kennedy became committed to being competitive in the Space Race. After careful consideration, Kennedy and Johnson decided they would have to land a man on the moon.

Getting the first human to the moon would be quite a challenge. Kennedy called Congress together in May of 1961, to ask for their support. Manned exploration of the moon, Kennedy argued, would help protect America's national security. It could also lead to important scientific discoveries. Several months later, he rallied the public to his side in a famous speech at Rice University. In front of thousands, Kennedy announced: "We choose to go to the moon. We choose to go to the moon in this decade and do the other things, not because they are easy, but because they are hard." The President pledged that the United States would not just win the Space Race, but also that America's success would be for the peace, security, and good of all people.

It was eight years before a human landed on the moon. During that time the Apollo program, NASA's attempt to make Kennedy's pledge come true, sent ten missions into space. Despite

setbacks, Apollo 11 landed on the moon on July 20th, 1969. American astronauts Neil Armstrong and Buzz Aldrin became the first humans to set foot on the moon. Their landing was broadcast live across the country. From the moon, Armstrong declared the landing to be "one small step for man, one giant leap for mankind."

President Kennedy did not witness this historic event. He had been assassinated two years after first pledging to land a man on the moon. However, because of his historic decision in 1961, the United States had succeeded in becoming the first country to send a human to the moon. America had won the Space Race.

Apolo Anton Ohno:
Decision Time

By Joey Dawson

It was 1998. The setting was a cabin in rainy, cold, and desolate Moclips, Washington. Apolo Anton Ohno, then age 15, had been left alone to think long and hard. He needed to make a difficult decision about his future as a short-track speed skater.

Short-track speed skating is a form of competitive speed skating on ice. Speed skating is an official Winter Olympic sport. Speed skaters race for a set number of laps around an oval ice rink. To be able to compete in the Olympic Winter Games, speed skaters need to make the official speed skating team for their country. For example, American speed skaters need to qualify at the U.S. Olympic trials.

Apolo grew up in Seattle, Washington. He was an only child who lived with his divorced father, Yuki. When Apolo was a young boy, he was an excellent inline skater. Apolo's speed and agility were outstanding. He was so good that he was encouraged to try speed skating. As a speed skater, Apolo had shown the potential to become a top competitor.

Apolo was accepted to train at the Olympic Training Center in Lake Placid, New York. This Training Center only invites young athletes with incredible promise because the training is very rigorous. Apolo was only thirteen when he had to move from Seattle to Lake Placid.

At first, Apolo was not happy at the Training Center. He wasn't ready to spend so much time training and refining his speed skating. His teammates nicknamed him "Chunky," but the teasing motivated Apolo to work harder.

Apolo began winning race after race. He broke two American speed skating records. At age 14, Apolo won the U.S. short-track speed skating championship.

But less than a year later, Apolo placed last at the U.S. Olympic trials. This meant he did not qualify for the 1998 Olympics. Once again, Apolo had lost his commitment to training.

When Apolo came in last place, his father was disappointed. But Yuki wasn't disappointed that Apolo lost. Instead, he was disappointed in Apolo's lack of effort.

Yuki decided it was time for his son to make a significant decision about his career. He drove Apolo to an area that they had visited many times in the past. It was a cabin in a remote location. It was so isolated that there was no television, no Internet, and no telephone access except for a pay phone located down the road.

Yuki left Apolo alone at the cabin. He wanted to give the boy time to consider his future. Yuki asked Apolo to choose one of two options: to pursue skating full-time or to quit and attend school instead. Yuki stressed that he would support whatever Apolo decided. He didn't care what the decision was; he wanted his son to come to terms with what his future would be.

Fifteen-year-old Apolo had to make an adult decision. Without anyone to talk to, he took long runs and trained by himself. He finally realized what he needed to do. Apolo called his father to say that he was ready to dedicate himself to speed skating.

Four years later, Apolo won silver and gold medals in the Winter Olympics. In the 2006 Olympics, he won three medals: gold, silver, and bronze. Apolo had made the right choice.

Minerva Hamilton Hoyt

By Amanda MacGregor

Minerva Hamilton Hoyt had a passion for gardening, a talent for organizing, and a concern for the deserts of California. This transplanted Southerner recognized that something needed to be done to protect the desert and set out to do something about it. She became an important environmental conservationist, most notably working tirelessly to create what is now Joshua Tree National Park.

Hoyt was born in Mississippi in 1866. She came to South Pasadena, California in the 1890s with her husband, Dr. Albert Sherman Hoyt. Minerva Hoyt became involved in numerous local charities. She also grew increasingly interested in gardening and in desert plants. At the time, many gardeners used native desert vegetation to enhance landscaping. The fad of cactus gardens led people to travel to the desert, where they would uproot mature cacti and other indigenous plants for their urban gardens, in some cases picking entire areas bare.

Westward expansion in a post-Gold Rush era was affecting the California deserts in other ways, too. Mining, ranching, and homesteading were quickly spreading through the region. Large numbers of automobiles were coming into the area on new roads, further threatening the environment. Population swelled as new railroad lines and the Panama Canal increased access to this

©satori13/iStockphoto.com

attractive part of the state. For Hoyt, this explosion of activity in southern California was worrisome. Her appreciation for the desert and its plants had grown even more over the years. Traveling through the area by wagon or horse, Hoyt enjoyed the beauty of cacti and Joshua trees, which she found magnificent. She reveled in the fact that these stunning plants could flourish in such a harsh climate. Hoyt was shocked by the damage she observed and resolved to protect the landscape from further destruction.

Hoyt began her crusade for desert protection by touring with an exhibit of desert plants. She displayed these at the 1928 Garden Club of America show in New York, and then went on to shows in other major cities. In 1930, Hoyt established the International Deserts Conservation League. Her goal was to create desert parks to protect the landscape and animals of southern California. A skilled organizer, Hoyt identified land that she hoped would be preserved, prepared reports, served on councils, and hired ecologists and biologists to help her in her quest.

She repeatedly addressed her requests to the National Park Service, but under President Hoover's leadership nothing happened. She was consulted in 1927, when landscape architect Frederick Law Olmsted Jr. was looking for desert state park sites. Hoyt suggested a park of more than one million acres, but her recommendations weren't used. It wasn't until President Franklin D. Roosevelt took office that Hoyt's projects started to move forward. The timing was perfect. Roosevelt's administration was looking for ways to create more jobs, and expanding national parks and monuments would do just that. In 1936, Roosevelt established the Joshua Tree National Monument, covering roughly 825,000 acres of land. Additionally, Hoyt aided in the creation of two other state parks, Death Valley and Anza-Borrego Desert, and convinced the Mexican government to create 10,000 acres of forest dedicated to cactus preservation.

Hoyt was determined to see her projects through and never gave up, constantly lobbying for conservation efforts. She died in 1945, never getting to see her park achieve the status she most hoped for. This happened in 1994, when President Bill Clinton signed the Desert Protection Act, which not only promoted Joshua Tree to a National Park, but also added 234,000 acres of land.

Today, Joshua Tree National Park is thriving, with more than 1.2 million visitors per year. There are self-guided nature trails, guided walking tours, and extensive dirt roads for cycling. Visitors to the park can enjoy rock climbing, picnicking, horseback riding, and camping. The park is home to abundant plant and animal diversity, with 750 species of plants, 45 species of reptiles, 52 species of mammals, and 250 species of birds.

It is thanks to Minerva Hoyt that this area of land has been allowed to flourish under protection. Today, there is a species of Mexican cactus named in her honor, a peak within Joshua Tree National Park named after her, and an annual Minerva Hoyt Award, given to others who work on behalf of California deserts. Her legacy lives on through these things and through the very existence of Joshua Tree National Park.

The park is home to abundant plant and animal diversity.

Althea Gibson

By Shauna Grant

All great athletes start somewhere. For Althea Gibson, that place was Harlem in the 1930s. Gibson honed her skills playing paddle tennis, a sort of cousin to the tennis popular today. By age 12, she was the New York City women's paddle-tennis champion. She would go on to become a tennis phenomenon, winning Wimbledon, the U.S. Nationals, and eleven Grand Slam titles. To do this, Gibson had to do something even harder than just win matches; she had to break the racial barrier.

Althea Gibson

Racism was everywhere in the United States in the 1940s and 1950s, and the sports world was no exception. Tennis was closed to minorities, with the United States Lawn Tennis Association having barred black players since its formation in 1881. Gibson began her rise to fame as a star player in the American Tennis Association (ATA) circuit. Despite being an outstanding player, she wasn't able to participate in tournaments outside of the ATA, an African American organization. This changed in 1950, when Gibson was invited to play in the United States National Championships, marking the first time an African American had competed in this tournament. The next year she became the first African American to compete at Wimbledon, an event she would go on to win repeatedly.

Gaining access to the exclusive world of tennis wasn't easy, but Gibson persevered and continued to break barriers, becoming the first African American to play in countless tournaments. But being allowed to compete didn't mean Gibson no longer faced prejudice. She was frequently denied access to restaurants or hotels. On the court, it often seemed that referees would cite Gibson for faults that white players weren't called for. Less skilled white players also received more invitations than Gibson, who felt her professional tennis career was stalling.

In her thirties, Gibson changed careers and broke the racial barrier again, this time in professional golf. In 1964, she became the first African American woman to participate in the Ladies Professional Golf Association tour. Most private country clubs banned African Americans, limiting Gibson's options for touring. If she was allowed to play, she often wasn't allowed in the locker rooms. As with tennis, Gibson persisted in spite of discrimination.

Gibson's pioneering success in the face of adversity left a permanent mark on sports history. Her determination to play and to push for inclusion paved the way for future athletes. Countless players who have followed in her footsteps have called Gibson an inspiration. Today, there are more minority tennis players than in the past. They have Althea Gibson to thank for her decisions, her courage, and her legacy.

Dr. Seuss and The Cat in the Hat

by Luz Appleby

The story of *The Cat in the Hat* starts on a rainy day with two bored kids at home. You might have read the book, or you might have seen the movie version. You might even have read other books by Dr. Seuss, including *Horton Hears a Who!* and *Green Eggs and Ham*. But do you know how Dr. Seuss came to write *The Cat in the Hat*? It all started with one very important decision—to write a book for children using only two hundred and thirty-six words.

Theodor Seuss Geisel, also known as Dr. Seuss, was born in Springfield, MA. As a teenager, he attended Dartmouth College. One of his activities included contributing to the school magazine, *The Jack-O-Lantern*. He used the pseudonym of "Seuss," which is his middle name and his mother's maiden name.

Geisel's first jobs were creating cartoons for newspapers, magazines, and advertising campaigns. He then started contributing weekly political cartoons to a magazine called *PM*. When America entered World War II, Geisel wanted to aid the war effort, even though he was too old to be drafted. He served in the U.S. Army's Information and Education Division. He learned about animation during his time with the U.S. Army, for his job was to create training movies.

Geisel continued his advertising work. He was contributing illustrations for quite a few magazines, when a publisher offered him a job illustrating a book of children's sayings. This assignment marked his first entrance into children's-book publishing. He received such high praise for his illustrations that he was inspired to write and illustrate his own book, *And to Think That I Saw It on Mulberry Street*.

At this time, the popular Dick and Jane books were used in most schools to teach reading. But many educators and critics proclaimed that these Dick and Jane books weren't effective for building literacy skills. The Dick and Jane books were based on a number of sight words, or words that children could memorize and recognize by sight, such as *and, or,* and *at.* Instead, educators believed that children would become better readers by learning phonics, which is sounding out the letters or sounds that groups of letters make. Many educators also agreed that children's books should be more entertaining.

William Spaulding, who was the head of Houghton Mifflin's education division, was one of these educators. He decided to do something completely radical and different. He asked Geisel to write a children's book—but he challenged Geisel to use only a very limited number of words that a first-grader would recognize. He said to Geisel, "Write me a story that first-graders can't put down!"

Geisel accepted the challenge. Spaulding sent him three different lists of words that had been compiled by experts. The first list was made up of two hundred and twenty words that first-graders would recognize by sight. The second list was made up of two hundred and twenty words that beginning readers would know from their phonics lessons, such as *sit* and *bit* and *jump* and *bump.* The third list was made up of words that first-graders might never have seen before but should be able to sound out, such as *shine* and

tricks. Geisel chose over two hundred words from these three lists, and added more of his own. He used only these two hundred and thirty-six words.

Geisel first decided to create a story from the first two words he saw that rhymed: *cat* and *hat.* Geisel continued to use a rhyming pattern throughout *The Cat in the Hat.* Using rhyming words was unusual in children's books, but it caught the attention of many children.

He then came up with an idea about a cat that visits two children during a rainy day. But this is no ordinary cat, for this cat can think and talk. He also has two mischievous friends called Thing 1 and Thing 2, and, together, they have silly and exciting adventures in misbehaving.

At the time, children were not used to reading about characters that misbehaved. (Some people thought that the characters were too rebellious and ridiculous!) Also, Geisel's brightly colored and imaginative illustrations were not like anything children had seen before. These young readers were completely excited by the amusing text and pictures!

And that is how *The Cat in the Hat* came to be.

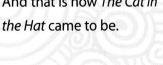

Decisions, decisions...

In life, you have to make decisions every day! How would you rate these decisions, in importance, according to YOU?

____ What to wear to school.

____ Going to camp or staying home during the summer.

____ Making healthy choices for lunch or eating what you like.

____ How long to study after school every day.

____ Who to invite to your birthday party.

____ What book to read next.

____ When to exercise and for how long.

____ In your time off: watching TV, hanging out with friends, or playing videogames.

What Tales Tell

Native American Storytelling

~ ♥ ~

The Aeneid Retold

~ ♥ ~

Storytelling in the Digital Age

~ ♥ ~

Learning from Fairy Tales

NATIVE AMERICAN STORYTELLING:
Creating Community Through Stories

by Casey Sullivan

Before Europeans arrived in North America, as many as ten million people were already living there and thriving off the land. These Native American societies were made up of many distinct communities. Their traditions varied widely from nation to nation and tribe to tribe. Each group was influenced by its environment and history. One thing, however, that connects different groups of Native Americans is the important role that storytelling plays in their cultures.

Storytelling in these cultures served as a form of education as well as entertainment. It was used to teach younger generations how to live in the world. Customs and traditions that developed over time were passed on to each generation through storytelling. Some customs might be symbolic, such as a ceremony that welcomes a youth into adulthood. Others could be practical, like a particular method of hunting or constructing shelter.

Stories were used to explain the importance, history, and purpose of such customs. The act of storytelling could incorporate singing, dancing, and musical instruments. For example, the Nanticoke tribe performed dances telling the stories of a hunter tracking a deer. In the dance, the deer spots the hunter and flees, and the hunter must continue the hunt until he is successful. Memorable stories made people feel connected to one another and ensured that important lessons would be learned.

Everyone wonders how things came to be the way they are. As children, we might have asked why the sky is blue, why birds fly and we don't, or why we have to go to school or do our chores. Stories can answer questions about why things are a particular way. For example, ravens and owls often fight. Why? In some Eskimo stories, Owl and Raven began as friends. Raven made a dress for Owl as a gift. But when it came time for Raven to tailor the dress to fit Owl, Raven would not stop hopping about. Owl grew angry and poured the oil from his lamp over Raven. Raven cried, "Caw! Caw!" as the burning oil turned him black. The two have fought ever since.

As we grow, we ask more complex questions. Why are we here? How did our world today come about? Many cultures answer these through creation myths, or stories that describe how and why the world came to be. Some of the most important types of stories Native Americans told were creation myths.

In Northern California, the Atsugewi Native Americans told the tale of how Silver-Fox created the world. In this story, Coyote and Silver-Fox lived in the sky, high above a world covered in water. Silver-Fox wanted to create other things, but Coyote objected. When Coyote was off running errands, Silver-Fox created a hole in the sky, climbed down, and made an island for himself. Coyote searched and found him, but the island was too small for the two of them. Silver-Fox made the land bigger so Coyote could have room to stretch out. Every day he enlarged the land, sending Coyote to run around the edge to see just how big it had grown. Silver-Fox then created the forests and animals and people. Today, coyotes still sneak around the edges of the world, looking to see how large the land has grown.

Native Americans told myths to explain not only the creation of the land itself, but other natural events as well. They passed down stories that explain why there is rain, why the sun rises and sets, where fire comes from, and other powerful acts of nature. Stories are a way to understand the world around us and to pass on that understanding.

Another vital purpose for storytelling is to teach values and good behavior. Just as fairy tales and fables teach children

about the consequences of their actions, so do many Native American stories. In one Native American story, a man had several wives whom he neglected, causing them to all fight. One day, a wife gave up and left, taking her son with her. Free from her husband and his other wives, she and her son grew large and happy—so large that they turned into mountains. A story like this teaches listeners about the importance of happiness, independence, and finding strength on your own.

Many Native American stories share similar characters and events. Many tribes or nations have stories about Raven, Coyote, or Buffalo. Whenever different tribes gather, they can share their stories and a bit of their own worlds. In this way, storytelling does not just tie together members of a single community, it helps people connect with those from other regions. Though many of these stories are now hundreds of years old, they continue to be told to this day, connecting whoever hears them to the Native American cultures of the past and present.

A Retelling of Virgil's

by Nicole Gee

Read about an ancient story that tells how the Roman Empire began.

Ancient Romans treasured Virgil's epic poem *The Aeneid*, which recounts the adventures and the ordeals of the hero Aeneas. Aeneas was the son of a Trojan, Anchises, and the goddess of beauty and love, Venus.

It was prophesied that Aeneas would found the city of Rome in Italy, and that his descendants would build the Roman Empire. But at the beginning of the story, Aeneas is leading a group of refugees and facing the anger of the queen of gods, Juno.

The Aeneid is made up of twelve books, or chapters. Book I begins *in medias res*, or in the middle of the plot. The Trojan War has been over for years. The Greeks defeated the Trojans and destroyed Troy. The Trojans fled their native land and are sailing across the Mediterranean Sea.

Aeneas and his fellow surviving Trojans have fled their homeland. They are now sailing on twenty ships to establish a new home in Italy.

86

(bg) ©Nella/Shutterstock; (tl) ©Comstock/Getty Images

The Aeneid, Book I

The goddess Juno commands the wind god Aeolus to create strong winds so that the Trojans will be caught in a storm and shipwrecked. Many of Aeneas's ships seem to be lost at sea.

The sea god Neptune calms the storm. Aeneas, along with several of his ships, manages to land in Carthage, a city on the African coast of the Mediterranean Sea.

Because the Trojans are now in an unfamiliar land, Jupiter, the king of gods, sends the messenger-god Mercury to the queen of Carthage, Dido. Mercury tells Dido and her people to be friendly to Aeneas and his companions.

Aeneas's mother Venus comes to Aeneas in a dream and tells him to go to the city and talk to Dido. Venus assures Aeneas that Dido will welcome the Trojans to Carthage. She also tells him that, if he asks for help in rebuilding his fleet, the queen will aid him.

Aeneas goes to Dido's temple. To his surprise, he finds the missing Trojans at the temple. He is now reunited with his friends.

Dido welcomes Aeneas and his crew to Carthage. She agrees to help Aeneas rebuild his fleet.

Which Fairy Tale

1. When you see that people are in need of urgent help, you

   a. immediately rush to save them without any hesitation.

   b. let someone else save the day, though you may help.

   c. make sure that everyone else is protected first.

2. When your friend is feeling upset, you

   a. listen while your friend expresses his or her feelings.

   b. cheer up your friend by joking, singing, or laughing.

   c. give advice to your friend.

3. When you need to make a big decision, do you

   a. confide in a trusted friend or mentor and ask for his or her guidance?

   b. find it easier to help others make decisions than to make decisions for yourself?

   c. not even think about the consequences before acting?

4. If you had magical powers, you would

  a. use your powers to help your family and your friends?

  b. hide your powers because you're not sure if they're powerful enough?

  c. use your powers to help a hero or heroine?

5. You are trying to complete a seemingly impossible and life-threatening task. You have never completed such an enormous task before. You

  a. keep trying until you complete it, because you are determined to succeed.

  b. find that you are afraid to complete it, because it seems too dangerous.

  c. find ways to complete the task by thinking practically and logically.

If You Chose Mostly

a. YOU ARE A HERO OR HEROINE. Your first instinct is to help those in need. You are brave and courageous. You enjoy spending time with your friends and your family. They trust you to have a strong heart and mind to lead them to safety or to fight when danger strikes. You are known for your quick intelligence. Notable heroes and heroines include: Hansel and Gretel, Cinderella, Mulan, Jack from *Jack and the Beanstalk,* Peter Pan, Robin Hood, and Aladdin from *Arabian Nights*.

b. YOU ARE A COMPANION WHO ADVISES THE HERO OR HEROINE. You usually accompany a hero or heroine on an adventure, because you believe in his or her cause. You are loyal and steadfast. You have earned their trust because of your noble qualities. Notable companions include: Enkidu from *The Epic of Gilgamesh,* the mice from *Cinderella,* Tinkerbell from *Peter Pan,* and Samwise Gamgee from *The Lord of the Rings*.

c. YOU ARE A MENTOR OR A TEACHER. You have the most powerful of magical abilities. You are wise and resourceful. You are widely revered and honored for your knowledge. Heroes and heroines often seek your wisdom, because they will need your knowledge to make an important decision about the adventures. You aid them in some important way so that they can be allowed to continue on their adventures. Notable mentors include: the fairy godmother from *Cinderella,* Gandalf from *The Lord of the Rings* series, Professor Dumbledore from the *Harry Potter* series, and Aslan from *The Chronicles of Narnia* series.

The Spread of Storytelling

by Amanda MacGregor

Humans have always participated in and valued oral and written storytelling. Whether it is tales passed on from generation to generation, or symbols and words scratched onto cave walls or stone tablets, storytelling has been an important part of our civilization since the beginning. Now, storytelling is more popular than ever. New technology and ways of creating connections have enabled more people to share stories. Stories hold power and meaning. They tie people together together, and they connect people to create communal experiences. Where are our modern-day storytellers? All over the internet.

Blogs, podcasts, videos, and social networks have enabled storytelling to remain at the forefront of our culture. These newer forms of storytelling have also allowed tales to reach increasingly widening audiences. People from all corners of the world can now enjoy each other's stories. This kind of sharing gives us a more global experience, highlighting our many similarities and teaching us about the ways in which we are different. Anyone with internet access and a little motivation can join the many voices from around the world. The tools needed to create blogs, podcasts, and videos are more accessible than ever. With endless innovations in how to produce and consume stories, digital storytelling allows creative expression in ways nearly unthinkable not that long ago.

Technology lets us interact with one another's stories and communicate directly with each other. We can leave comments on a blog or video, follow other people, and engage in conversation with both the content creator and other viewers. We're even changing how we see our world, with people focusing on the things around them to find a good story

in the Digital Age

to share. With digital storytelling, we can see expressions and gestures, hear inflections, and see pictures. That's not dissimilar to oral and written storytelling of the past, when stories were often told or read aloud. The best part of modern storytelling? We can share stories with just one click.

The more things change, the more they stay the same. The tradition of storytelling defines and unites us, and modern storytellers will continue to redefine how a story is shared. We may not be sitting in a circle around an elder or reading stone tablets, but stories are still revealing our experiences and bringing us closer together. The tools may be different, but the message is the same as it's always been: stories matter.

What You Can Learn from Fairy Tales

Remember the stories you read as a kid? They all had lessons to teach. Let's see how well you remember them! Read these clues and match them with the title of the fairy tale and its moral or lesson.

1.

CLUES A boy and his sister live in the middle of the deep woods with their kind father and mean stepmother. This evil woman has a terrible plan. She will lead her two stepchildren into the woods in the dark of night. Then she will run away, leaving them alone!

However, the boy guesses her plan. Before they leave their cottage, he stuffs his pockets with white pebbles.

(He knows that they will shine in the moonlight.) As the three walk through the woods, the boy secretly drops the pebbles along their path. When the evil, cackling stepmother runs away and hides from the children, they wait a safe amount of time, and then they follow the pebble path back home, where their worried father welcomes them.

What is the story? _____
What is the moral of this story? _____

2.

CLUE This special animal family returns home from their regular walk in the woods. When they open the door of their house, they make an unpleasant discovery!

Someone has been in their house, eaten their food, broken their furniture, and slept in their beds. The angry bear family decides to find and punish the culprit.

What is the story? _____
What is the moral of this story? _____

94

(bkgd) ©WELBURNSTUART/Shutterstock; (cr) ©Jupiterimages/Getty Images; (bl) ©Anton Brand/Shutterstock

3. **CLUE** After a young woman's beloved mother dies, her father remarries. The new wife is very mean, and she has two mean daughters. All three treat the motherless young woman badly, making her life miserable. She continues to work hard, cleaning the fireplace and scrubbing the floors. She is always sweet, always kind.

One day, the prince of the land spots this lovely young woman and falls madly in love with her! However, he then loses sight of her. Not knowing her name or where she lives, the determined prince searches everywhere. Finally, at long last, he finds his beloved. They marry and live happily ever after.

What is the story? _____
What is the moral of this story? _____

4. **CLUE** The queen of an ancient land gives birth to a baby girl. The king and queen hold a grand feast to honor the newborn princess. However, the staff forgets to invite the kingdom's most important fairy to the grand feast. The queen makes up a pitiful excuse. She claims not to have enough dishes to include this fairy.

The forgotten fairy is enraged that she was excluded from the feast. She is even angrier when she hears the queen's sorry excuse. To pay back the queen, the fairy puts a curse on the baby. Years later, the grownup princess pricks her finger and falls into a deep sleep. Her frantic parents try to waken her. They do not succeed.

Then one day, years later, a wealthy, handsome prince kisses the beautiful princess, and she awakens! The kingdom and all of its people rejoice! All, that is, except for the miserable fairy!

What is the story? _____
What is the moral of this story? _____

5. **CLUE** A girl and her mother live in a small cottage in the woods. One day, the mother says, "Daughter, take this basket of goodies to your grandma. She is ill and has nothing to eat." The girl nods and promises that she will. Just before the girl leaves, her mother warns her, "Stay on the path! Do not stop until you get to Grandma's house. And do not talk with strangers! Not today! Not ever!"

On her way to Grandma's house, a wolf stops to chat with the girl. But the wolf does not look like a wolf!

In no time at all, the girl informs the wolf where her grandma lives. She explains that she is sick in bed and has no food. Hurrying ahead, the wolf arrives at the grandmother's house and eats her up! In some versions of the story, the girl meets the same fate.

What is the story? _____
What is the moral of this story? _____

6. **CLUE** A small, homely bird hatches in a shelter in the barnyard. All of the other animals begin to make fun of the scrawny bird, calling him names.

As a result, the poor little bird is always very sad. Every day, he wanders around the barnyard, looking for a friend, but no animal wants to befriend him. When winter comes, the lake freezes and the little bird is even colder. He feels even more alone as he watches the wild swans take flight. "If only I could be like them," he says to himself.

As the spring sunshine begins to warm the barnyard, the little bird once again looks up to see the beautiful swans and ducks flying across the sky. "If only I could do that," he says to himself. "If only I looked like these swans, maybe others would like me." Then one day, little by little, the little bird begins to change. His stubby wings start to grow. The color of his dusty feathers changes to a shiny white. They glisten in the bright sun. Before long, the once-ugly bird is acclaimed to be the most beautiful bird in the farmyard.

What is the story? _____
What is the moral of this story? _____

FAIRY TALES	**MORALS**
Goldilocks and the Three Bears	Don't be afraid to be yourself!
Cinderella	Be prepared! Know your enemies!
Hansel and Gretel	Love is a powerful force in our world!
The Ugly Duckling	To be safe from harm, children must obey their parents.
Sleeping Beauty	Never give up! Good fortune may find you!
Little Red Riding Hood	Respect the property and privacy of others.

1. Hansel and Gretel: Be prepared! Know your enemies! 2. Goldilocks and the Three Bears: Respect the property and privacy of others. 3. Cinderella: Never give up! Good fortune may find you! 4. Sleeping Beauty: Love is a powerful force in our world! 5. Little Red Riding Hood: To be safe from harm, children must obey their parents. 6. The Ugly Duckling: Don't be afraid to be yourself!